This book belongs to:
Joanne Maclean

Farmyard Animals

Written by Paula Borton
Illustrated by Lisa Alderson

This is a Parragon book
First published in 2003

Copyright © Parragon 2003

Parragon
Queen Street House
4 Queen Street
Bath BA1 1HE, UK

ISBN 1-40541-879-6

Farmyard Animals

p

Contents

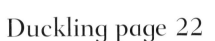

Cow

Cow lives in the meadow. She has a smooth, leathery coat. Her tail keeps the flies away.

Moo!

Milk comes from Cow's udders.

Cow chews grass all day.

Cow's baby is called a calf.

When Cow sleeps, she lies down on her side.

   9

Calf

Calf is a baby cow. When she is born, her mummy licks her clean. Calf can walk almost as soon as she is born.
Her legs are a bit wobbly to start with!

Moo!

Calf and her mummy
sniff each other.
They know each
other's smell.

Calf's daddy is a bull.

Calf sucks her
mummy's milk.

Sheep

Sheep lives on the hillside. She has a thick, woolly coat to keep her warm. Sheep can jump and climb. Can you see her hoofs?

Baa!

Sheep has her woolly coat cut every summer. It grows back by winter.

Sheep's baby is called a lamb.

We use Sheep's wool to make clothes.

Sheep eats grass.

   13

Lamb

Lamb is a baby sheep. Her woolly coat keeps her warm out in the field. Look at her long tail and dainty hoofs.

Baa!

Lamb can stand and walk
as soon as she is born.

Lamb drinks her
mummy's milk.

Baa!

Baa!

If Lamb is lost, she
listens for her mummy's
call, "Baa!"

Hen

Hen lives in the farmyard.
She has colourful
feathers. Can you see
the bright red comb
on her head?

Cluck!

Hen pecks with her beak looking for seeds and insects.

Hen scratches the ground with her claws looking for food.

Hen's babies are called chicks.

Hen lays eggs.
We eat some hens' eggs.

Chick

Chick's mummy is a hen. Chick hatches from an egg. Look at her soft, fluffy feathers and her tiny beak.

Cheep!

Chick's daddy
is a cockerel.

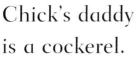

Cock-a-doodle-doo!

Chick grows
inside
an egg.

Chick breaks out of
the egg when she
is ready to
be born.

Duck

Duck lives on the pond.
Look at her webbed feet.
Duck has a yellow beak
and soft white feathers.

   20

Duck can fly as well as swim and waddle!

A baby duck is a duckling.

Duck eats worms and weeds.

Duck uses her webbed feet to push through the water.

Duckling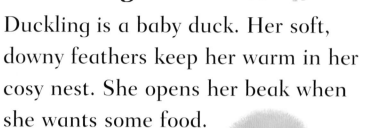

Duckling is a baby duck. Her soft,
downy feathers keep her warm in her
cosy nest. She opens her beak when
she wants some food.

Quack!

Duckling hatches from an egg.
When she is three weeks old,
Duckling's grown-up feathers
start to grow.

Duckling can swim straight away
paddling with her webbed feet.

Pig

Pig lives in a sty. She has small eyes and a stubby nose. Can you see her curly tail?

Oink!

Pig rolls around in the mud to keep cool.

Pig snuffles in the ground to find her favourite food – vegetable roots.

The mummy pig is called a sow. Her babies are called piglets.

   25

Piglet

Piglet is a baby pig. Piglet has smooth skin, perky ears and a wriggly tail. And lots of noisy brothers and sisters.

Oink!

Piglet sleeps a lot when she is first born.

Piglet pushes her brothers and sisters to get her share of milk.

Piglet copies her mummy, searching for food with her small, stubby snout.

Horse

Horse lives in the field.
She has a smooth, shiny coat
and a long mane and tail.

Neigh!

The mummy horse is called a mare. Her baby is called a foal.

Horse eats grass and hay.

Horse can gallop very fast!

Foal

Foal is a baby horse. She can run about just a few hours after being born!
Foal swishes her tail to keep flies away. Look at her long legs!

Neigh!

Foal's daddy is a stallion.

Foal drinks her
mummy's milk
until she is
six months old.

Foal loves to roll about on the grass!

   31

Goodbye!